On this Day - August 1ˢᵗ

By

Kerry Butters

August 1st.

August 1 is the 213th day of the year (214th in leap years) in the Gregorian calendar. There are 152 days remaining until the end of the year. This date is slightly more likely to fall on a Monday, Wednesday or Saturday (58 in 400 years each) than on Thursday or Friday (57), and slightly less likely to occur on a Tuesday or Sunday (56).

Contents

Events

- 30 BC – Octavian (later known as Augustus) enters Alexandria, Egypt, bringing it under the control of the Roman Republic.
- 69 – Batavian rebellion: The Batavians in Germania Inferior (Netherlands) revolt under the leadership of Gaius Julius Civilis.
- 527 – Justinian I becomes the sole ruler of the Byzantine Empire.
- 607 – Ono no Imoko is dispatched as envoy to the Sui court in China (Traditional Japanese date: July 3, 607).
- 902 – Taormina, the last Byzantine stronghold in Sicily, is captured by the Aghlabids army, concluding the Muslim conquest of Sicily.
- 1203 – Isaac II Angelos, restored Eastern Roman Emperor, declares his son Alexios IV Angelos co-emperor after pressure from the forces of the Fourth Crusade.
- 1291 – The Old Swiss Confederacy is formed with the signature of the Federal Charter.

- 1469 – Louis XI of France founds the chivalric order called the Order of Saint Michael in Amboise.
- 1498 – Christopher Columbus becomes the first European to visit what is now Venezuela.
- 1620 – The Speedwell leaves Delfshaven to bring pilgrims to America by way of England.
- 1664 – Ottoman forces are defeated in the battle of Saint Gotthard by an Austrian army led by Raimondo Montecuccoli, resulting in the Peace of Vasvár.
- 1714 – George, Elector of Hanover, becomes King George I of Great Britain, marking the beginning of the Georgian era of British history.
- 1715 – The Riot Act comes into force in England.
- 1759 – Seven Years' War: The Battle of Minden, an allied Anglo-German army victory over the French. In Britain this was one of a number of events that constituted the Annus Mirabilis of 1759 and is celebrated as Minden Day by certain British Army regiments.
- 1774 – British scientist Joseph Priestley discovers oxygen gas, corroborating the prior discovery of this element by German-Swedish chemist Carl Wilhelm Scheele.
- 1798 – French Revolutionary Wars: Battle of the Nile (Battle of Aboukir Bay): Battle begins when a British fleet engages the French Revolutionary Navy fleet in an unusual night action.

- 1800 – The Acts of Union 1800 is passed in which merges the Kingdom of Great Britain and the Kingdom of Ireland into the United Kingdom of Great Britain and Ireland.
- 1801 – First Barbary War: The American schooner USS *Enterprise* captures the Tripolitan polacca *Tripoli* in a single-ship action off the coast of modern-day Libya.
- 1831 – A new London Bridge opens.
- 1834 – Slavery is abolished in the British Empire as the Slavery Abolition Act 1833 comes into force.
- 1838 – Non-laborer slaves in most of the British Empire are emancipated.
- 1840 – Laborer slaves in most of the British Empire are emancipated.
- 1842 – The Lombard Street riot erupts in Philadelphia, Pennsylvania, United States.
- 1855 – The first ascent of Monte Rosa, the second highest summit in the Alps.
- 1876 – Colorado is admitted as the 38th U.S. state.
- 1894 – The First Sino-Japanese War erupts between Japan and China over Korea.
- 1907 – The start of the first Scout camp on Brownsea Island, the origin of the worldwide Scouting movement.
- 1911 – Harriet Quimby takes her pilot's test and becomes the first U.S. woman to earn an Aero Club of America aviator's certificate.

- 1914 – The German Empire declares war on the Russian Empire at the opening of World War I. The Swiss Army mobilizes because of World War I.
- 1927 – The Nanchang Uprising marks the first significant battle in the Chinese Civil War between the Kuomintang and Chinese Communist Party. This day is commemorated as the anniversary of the founding of the People's Liberation Army.
- 1937 – Josip Broz Tito reads the resolution "Manifesto of constitutional congress of KPH" to the constitutive congress of KPH (Croatian Communist Party) in woods near Samobor.
- 1944 – World War II: The Warsaw Uprising against the Nazi occupation breaks out in Warsaw, Poland.
- 1946 – Leaders of the Russian Liberation Army, a force of Russian prisoners of war that collaborated with Nazi Germany, are executed in Moscow, Soviet Union for treason.
- 1957 – The United States and Canada form the North American Aerospace Defense Command (NORAD).
- 1960 – Dahomey (later renamed Benin) declares independence from France.
- 1960 – Islamabad is declared the federal capital of the Government of Pakistan.
- 1961 – U.S. Defense Secretary Robert McNamara orders the creation of the Defense Intelligence Agency (DIA), the nation's first centralized military espionage organization.

- 1964 – The former Belgian Congo is renamed the Democratic Republic of the Congo.
- 1966 – Charles Whitman kills 16 people at the University of Texas at Austin before being killed by the police.
- 1966 – Purges of intellectuals and imperialists becomes official China policy at the beginning of the Cultural Revolution.
- 1968 – The coronation is held of Hassanal Bolkiah, the 29th Sultan of Brunei.
- 1974 – Cyprus dispute: The United Nations Security Council authorizes the UNFICYP to create the "Green Line", dividing Cyprus into two zones.
- 1975 – CSCE Final Act creates the Conference for Security and Co-operation in Europe.
- 1980 – Vigdís Finnbogadóttir is elected President of Iceland and becomes the world's first democratically elected female head of state.
- 1980 – A train crash kills 18 people in County Cork, Ireland.
- 1981 – MTV begins broadcasting in the United States and airs its first video, "Video Killed the Radio Star" by The Buggles.
- 1984 – Commercial peat-cutters discover the preserved bog body of a man, called Lindow Man, at Lindow Moss, Cheshire, northwest England
- 1993 – The Great Mississippi and Missouri Rivers Flood of 1993 comes to a peak.

- 2001 – Alabama Supreme Court Chief Justice Roy Moore has a Ten Commandments monument installed in the judiciary building, leading to a lawsuit to have it removed and his own removal from office.
- 2004 – A supermarket fire kills 396 people and injures 500 others in Asunción, Paraguay.
- 2007 – The I-35W Mississippi River bridge spanning the Mississippi River in Minneapolis, Minnesota, collapses during the evening rush hour.
- 2008 – The Beijing–Tianjin Intercity Railway begins operation as the fastest commuter rail system in the world.
- 2008 – Eleven mountaineers from international expeditions died on K2, the second-highest mountain on Earth in the worst single accident in the history of K2 mountaineering.
- 2010 – Convention on Cluster Munitions enters into force.
- 2014 – Convention on preventing and combating violence against women and domestic violence enters into force.

Births

- 10 BC – Claudius, Roman emperor (d. 54)
- 126 – Pertinax, Roman emperor (d. 193)
- 845 – Sugawara no Michizane, Japanese scholar and politician (d. 903)

- 1068 – Emperor Taizu of Jin (d. 1123)
- 1313 – Emperor Kōgon of Japan (d. 1364)
- 1377 – Emperor Go-Komatsu of Japan (d. 1433)
- 1545 – Andrew Melville, Scottish theologian and scholar (d. 1622)
- 1555 – Edward Kelley, English occultist (d. 1597)
- 1579 – Luis Vélez de Guevara, Spanish author and playwright (d. 1644)
- 1626 – Sabbatai Zevi, Montenegrin rabbi and theorist (d. 1676)
- 1630 – Thomas Clifford, 1st Baron Clifford of Chudleigh, English politician, Lord High Treasurer (d. 1673)
- 1659 – Sebastiano Ricci, Italian painter (d. 1734)
- 1713 – Charles I, Duke of Brunswick-Wolfenbüttel (d. 1780)
- 1714 – Richard Wilson, Welsh painter and academic (d. 1782)
- 1738 – Jacques François Dugommier, French general (d. 1794)
- 1744 – Jean-Baptiste Lamarck, French soldier, biologist, and academic (d. 1829)
- 1770 – William Clark, American soldier, explorer, and politician, 4th Governor of Missouri Territory (d. 1838)
- 1779 – Francis Scott Key, American lawyer, author, and poet (d. 1843)

- 1779 – Lorenz Oken, German-Swiss botanist, biologist, and ornithologist (d. 1851)
- 1809 – William B. Travis, American colonel and lawyer (d. 1836)
- 1815 – Richard Henry Dana, Jr., American lawyer and politician (d. 1882)
- 1818 – Maria Mitchell, American astronomer and academic (d. 1889)
- 1819 – Herman Melville, American novelist, short story writer, and poet (d. 1891)
- 1831 – Antonio Cotogni, Italian opera singer and educator (d. 1918)
- 1843 – Robert Todd Lincoln, American lawyer and politician, 35th United States Secretary of War (d. 1926)
- 1856 – George Coulthard, Australian footballer and cricketer (d. 1883)
- 1858 – Gaston Doumergue, French lawyer and politician, 13th President of France (d. 1937)
- 1858 – Hans Rott, Austrian organist and composer (d. 1884)
- 1861 – Sammy Jones, Australian cricketer (d. 1951)
- 1871 – John Lester, American cricketer and soccer player (d. 1969)
- 1877 – George Hackenschmidt, Estonian-English wrestler and strongman (d. 1968)
- 1881 – Otto Toeplitz, German mathematician and academic (d. 1940)

- 1885 – George de Hevesy, Hungarian-German chemist and academic, Nobel Prize laureate (d. 1966)
- 1889 – Walter Gerlach, German physicist and academic (d. 1979)
- 1891 – Karl Kobelt, Swiss lawyer and politician, 52nd President of the Swiss Confederation (d. 1968)
- 1893 – Alexander of Greece (d. 1920)
- 1894 – Ottavio Bottecchia, Italian cyclist (d. 1927)
- 1899 – Raymond Mays, English race car driver and businessman (d. 1980)
- 1900 – Otto Nothling, Australian cricketer and rugby player (d. 1965)
- 1901 – Francisco Guilledo, Filipino boxer (d. 1925)
- 1903 – Paul Horgan, American historian, author, and academic (d. 1995)
- 1905 – Helen Sawyer Hogg, American-Canadian astronomer and academic (d. 1993)
- 1907 – Eric Shipton, Sri Lankan-English mountaineer and explorer (d. 1977)
- 1910 – James Henry Govier, English painter and illustrator (d. 1974)
- 1910 – Mohammad Nissar, Indian cricketer (d. 1963)
- 1910 – Walter Scharf, American pianist and composer (d. 2003)
- 1911 – Jackie Ormes, American journalist and cartoonist (d. 1985)
- 1912 – Gego, German-Venezuelan sculptor and academic (d. 1994)

- 1912 – Henry Jones, American actor (d. 1999)
- 1914 – Jack Delano, American photographer and composer (d. 1997)
- 1914 – Alan Moore, Australian painter and educator (d. 2015)
- 1914 – J. Lee Thompson, English-Canadian director, producer, and screenwriter (d. 2002)
- 1916 – Fiorenzo Angelini, Italian cardinal (d. 2014)
- 1916 – Anne Hébert, Canadian author and poet (d. 2000)
- 1918 – T. J. Jemison, American minister and activist (d. 2013)
- 1918 – Richard Pearson, Welsh-English actor (d. 2011)
- 1919 – Stanley Middleton, English author (d. 2009)
- 1920 – Raul Renter, Estonian economist and chess player (d. 1992)
- 1920 – Jeffrey Segal, English actor (d.2015)
- 1921 – Jack Kramer, American tennis player, sailor, and sportscaster (d. 2009)
- 1921 – Pat McDonald, Australian actress (d. 1990)
- 1922 – Arthur Hill, Canadian-American actor (d. 2006)
- 1923 – Val Bettin, American actor
- 1924 – Marcia Mae Jones, American actress and singer (d. 2007)
- 1924 – Abdullah of Saudi Arabia (d. 2015)
- 1924 – Frank Worrell, Barbadian cricketer (d. 1967)
- 1925 – Ernst Jandl, Austrian poet and author (d. 2000)
- 1926 – Theo Adam, German opera singer

- 1926 – George Hauptfuhrer, American basketball player and lawyer (d. 2013)
- 1927 – Anthony G. Bosco, American bishop (d. 2013)
- 1928 – Jack Shea, American director, producer, and screenwriter (d. 2013)
- 1929 – Hafizullah Amin, Afghan educator and politician, Afghan Minister of Foreign Affairs (d. 1979)
- 1929 – Ann Calvello, American roller derby racer (d. 2006)
- 1930 – Lionel Bart, English composer (d. 1999)
- 1930 – Pierre Bourdieu, French sociologist, anthropologist, and philosopher (d. 2002)
- 1930 – Julie Bovasso, American actress and writer (d. 1991)
- 1930 – Lawrence Eagleburger, American lieutenant and politician, 62nd United States Secretary of State (d. 2011)
- 1930 – Károly Grósz, Hungarian politician, 51st Prime Minister of Hungary (d. 1996)
- 1930 – Geoffrey Holder, Trinidadian-American actor, singer, dancer, and choreographer (d. 2014)
- 1931 – Ramblin' Jack Elliott, American singer-songwriter and guitarist
- 1931 – Trevor Goddard, South African cricketer
- 1932 – Meir Kahane, American-Israeli rabbi and activist, founded the Jewish Defense League (d. 1990)
- 1932 – Meena Kumari, Indian actress (d. 1972)

- 1933 – Dom DeLuise, American actor, singer, director, and producer (d. 2009)
- 1933 – Masaichi Kaneda, Japanese baseball player and manager
- 1933 – Teri Shields, American actress, producer, and agent (d. 2012)
- 1933 – Dušan Třeštík, Czech historian and author (d. 2007)
- 1934 – John Beck, New Zealand cricketer (d. 2000)
- 1934 – Derek Birdsall, English graphic designer
- 1935 – Geoff Pullar, English cricketer (d. 2014)
- 1936 – W. D. Hamilton, Egyptian-English biologist, psychologist, and academic (d. 2000)
- 1936 – Yves Saint Laurent, Algerian-French fashion designer, co-founded Yves Saint Laurent (d. 2008)
- 1936 – Laurie Taylor, English sociologist, radio host, and academic
- 1937 – Al D'Amato, American lawyer and politician
- 1939 – Bob Frankford, English-Canadian physician and politician (d. 2015)
- 1939 – Terry Kiser, American actor
- 1939 – Stephen Sykes, English bishop and theologian (d. 2014)
- 1939 – Robert James Waller, American author and photographer
- 1940 – Mervyn Kitchen, English cricketer and umpire
- 1940 – Ram Loevy, Israeli director and screenwriter

- 1940 – Henry Silverman, American businessman, founded the Cendant Corporation
- 1941 – Ron Brown, American captain and politician, 30th United States Secretary of Commerce (d. 1996)
- 1941 – Étienne Roda-Gil, French songwriter and screenwriter (d. 2004)
- 1942 – Jerry Garcia, American singer-songwriter and guitarist (Grateful Dead, Legion of Mary, Old and in the Way, and New Riders of the Purple Sage) (d. 1995)
- 1942 – Giancarlo Giannini, Italian actor, director, producer, and screenwriter
- 1944 – Dmitry Nikolayevich Filippov, Russian banker and politician (d. 1998)
- 1944 – Andrew G. Vajna, Hungarian-American film producer
- 1945 – Douglas Osheroff, American physicist and academic, Nobel Prize laureate
- 1946 – Boz Burrell, English singer-songwriter and guitarist (King Crimson and Bad Company) (d. 2006)
- 1946 – Rick Coonce, American drummer (The Grass Roots) (d. 2011)
- 1946 – Richard O. Covey, American colonel, pilot, and astronaut
- 1946 – Fiona Stanley, Australian epidemiologist and academic
- 1947 – Lorna Goodison, Jamaican poet and author

- 1948 – Avi Arad, Israeli-American screenwriter and producer, founded Marvel Studios
- 1948 – Cliff Branch, American football player
- 1948 – David Gemmell, English journalist and author (d. 2006)
- 1949 – Kurmanbek Bakiyev, Kyrgyzstani politician, 2nd President of Kyrgyzstan
- 1949 – Jim Carroll, American poet and author (d. 2009)
- 1949 – Ray Nettles, American football player (d. 2009)
- 1950 – Bunkhouse Buck, American wrestler
- 1950 – Roy Williams, American basketball player and coach
- 1951 – Tim Bachman, Canadian singer and guitarist (Bachman–Turner Overdrive and Brave Belt)
- 1951 – Tommy Bolin, American singer-songwriter and guitarist (Deep Purple, Zephyr, and James Gang) (d. 1976)
- 1951 – Pete Mackanin, American baseball player, coach, and manager
- 1952 – Zoran Đinđić, Serbian philosopher and politician, 6th Prime Minister of Serbia (d. 2003)
- 1952 – Yajurvindra Singh, Indian cricketer
- 1953 – Robert Cray, American singer and guitarist
- 1953 – Howard Kurtz, American journalist and author
- 1954 – Trevor Berbick, Jamaican-Canadian boxer (d. 2006)
- 1954 – James Gleick, American journalist and author

- 1954 – Benno Möhlmann, German footballer and manager
- 1955 – Arun Lal, Indian cricketer and sportscaster
- 1956 – Ku Ok-hee, South Korean golfer (d. 2013)
- 1956 – Lewis Smith, American actor
- 1957 – Taylor Negron, American actor and screenwriter (d. 2015)
- 1958 – Rob Buck, American guitarist and songwriter (10,000 Maniacs) (d. 2000)
- 1958 – Michael Penn, American singer-songwriter and guitarist (Doll Congress)
- 1958 – Kiki Vandeweghe, American basketball player and coach
- 1959 – Joe Elliott, English singer-songwriter, guitarist, and producer (Def Leppard, Atomic Mass, and Down 'n' Outz)
- 1959 – Otomo Yoshihide, Japanese guitarist and songwriter (Ground Zero and Filament)
- 1960 – Chuck D, American rapper and producer (Public Enemy, The Bomb Squad, and Confrontation Camp)
- 1960 – Suzi Gardner, American singer-songwriter and guitarist (L7)
- 1960 – Professor Griff, American rapper (Public Enemy and Confrontation Camp)
- 1962 – Jesse Borrego, American actor and singer
- 1962 – Jacob Matlala, South African boxer (d. 2013)

- 1963 – Coolio, American rapper, producer, and actor (WC and the Maad Circle)
- 1963 – Demián Bichir, Mexican-American actor and producer
- 1963 – John Carroll Lynch, American actor
- 1963 – Lynette Sadleir, New Zealand swimmer
- 1963 – Koichi Wakata, Japanese astronaut and engineer
- 1963 – Dean Wareham, New Zealand singer-songwriter and guitarist (Galaxie 500, Luna, and Dean & Britta)
- 1964 – Adam Duritz, American singer-songwriter and producer (Counting Crows and The Himalayans)
- 1964 – Kaspar Capparoni, Italian actor
- 1964 – Fiona Hyslop, Scottish businesswoman and politician
- 1965 – Brandt Jobe, American golfer
- 1965 – Sam Mendes, English director and producer
- 1966 – George Ducas, American singer-songwriter and guitarist
- 1966 – James St. James, American club promoter and author
- 1967 – Gregg Jefferies, American baseball player and coach
- 1967 – José Padilha, Brazilian director, producer and screenwriter
- 1968 – Stacey Augmon, American basketball player and coach

- 1968 – Dan Donegan, American guitarist (Disturbed, Fight or Flight, and Vandal)
- 1968 – Shigetoshi Hasegawa, Japanese baseball player and sportscaster
- 1969 – Andrei Borissov, Estonian footballer and manager
- 1969 – Kevin Jarvis, American baseball player and scout
- 1969 – Graham Thorpe, English cricketer and journalist
- 1969 – David Wain, American actor, director, and screenwriter
- 1970 – Sibel Can, Turkish singer, actress, and dancer
- 1970 – Quentin Coryatt, American football player
- 1970 – David James, English footballer and manager
- 1970 – Elon Lindenstrauss, Israeli mathematician and academic
- 1971 – Jorge Eduardo Costilla Sánchez, Mexican drug lord
- 1971 – Ágúst Gylfason, Icelandic footballer
- 1971 – Charles Malik Whitfield, American actor and producer
- 1971 – İdil Üner, German-Turkish actress and singer
- 1972 – Nicke Andersson, Swedish singer-songwriter and guitarist (The Hellacopters The Solution, The Hydromatics, and Imperial State Electric)
- 1972 – Christer Basma, Norwegian footballer and coach

- 1972 – Todd Bouman, American football player and coach
- 1972 – Martin Damm, Czech-American tennis player
- 1972 – Devon Hughes, American wrestler and trainer
- 1972 – Thomas Woods, American historian, economist, and academic
- 1973 – Gregg Berhalter, American soccer player and coach
- 1973 – Veerle Dejaeghere, Belgian runner
- 1973 – Kris Holden-Ried, Canadian actor
- 1973 – Eduardo Noriega, Spanish actor
- 1973 – Edurne Pasaban, Spanish mountaineer
- 1974 – Cher Calvin, American journalist
- 1974 – Marek Galiński, Polish cyclist (d. 2014)
- 1974 – Tyron Henderson, South African cricketer
- 1974 – Dennis Lawrence, Trinidadian footballer and coach
- 1974 – Beckie Scott, Canadian skier
- 1975 – Vhrsti, Czech author and illustrator
- 1975 – Håkon Mjåset Johansen, Norwegian drummer and composer (Motif and Come Shine)
- 1975 – Teresa Mak, Hong Kong actress
- 1975 – Ryoko Yonekura, Japanese model and actress
- 1976 – Don Hertzfeldt, American animator, producer, screenwriter, and voice actor
- 1976 – Søren Jochumsen, Danish footballer
- 1976 – Nwankwo Kanu, Nigerian footballer

- 1976 – David Nemirovsky, Canadian ice hockey player
- 1976 – Hasan Şaş, Turkish footballer and manager
- 1976 – Cristian Stoica, Romanian-Italian rugby player
- 1977 – Marc Denis, Canadian ice hockey player and sportscaster
- 1977 – Haspop, French-Moroccan dancer, choreographer, and actor
- 1977 – Darnerien McCants, American-Canadian football player
- 1977 – Damien Saez, French singer-songwriter and guitarist
- 1977 – Yoshi Tatsu, Japanese wrestler and boxer
- 1978 – Andy Blignaut, Zimbabwean cricketer
- 1978 – Björn Ferry, Swedish biathlete
- 1978 – Dhani Harrison, English singer-songwriter and guitarist (Thenewno2, Traveling Wilburys, and Fistful of Mercy)
- 1978 – Chris Iwelumo, Scottish footballer
- 1978 – Edgerrin James, American football player
- 1979 – Junior Agogo, Ghanaian footballer
- 1979 – Nathan Fien, Australian-New Zealand rugby player
- 1979 – Jason Momoa, American actor, director, and producer
- 1980 – Mancini, Brazilian footballer
- 1980 – Romain Barras, French decathlete
- 1980 – Esteban Paredes, Chilean footballer

- 1981 – Ashley Parker Angel, American singer-songwriter, guitarist, and actor (O-Town)
- 1981 – Dean Cox, Australian footballer
- 1981 – Vaiko Eplik, Estonian singer-songwriter guitarist, and producer
- 1981 – Taylor Fry, American actress
- 1981 – Pia Haraldsen, Norwegian journalist and author
- 1981 – Christofer Heimeroth, German footballer
- 1981 – Stephen Hunt, Irish footballer
- 1981 – Jamie Jones-Buchanan, English rugby player
- 1982 – Basem Fathi, Jordanian footballer
- 1982 – Montserrat Lombard, English actress, director, and screenwriter
- 1982 – Ai Tominaga, Japanese model and actress
- 1983 – Bobby Carpenter, American football player
- 1983 – Craig Clarke, New Zealand rugby player
- 1983 – Julien Faubert, French footballer
- 1983 – David Gervasi, Swiss decathlete
- 1984 – Steve Feak, American game designer
- 1984 – Francesco Gavazzi, Italian cyclist
- 1984 – Brandon Kintzler, American baseball player
- 1984 – Valery Ortiz, Puerto Rican-American actress and singer
- 1984 – Bastian Schweinsteiger, German footballer
- 1985 – Stuart Holden, Scottish-American soccer player
- 1985 – Adam Jones, American baseball player
- 1985 – Hyun Jyu-ni, South Korean singer and actress

- 1985 – Cole Kimball, American baseball player
- 1985 – Gegard Mousasi, Iranian-Dutch mixed martial artist and kick-boxer
- 1985 – Tendai Mtawarira, South African rugby player
- 1985 – Kris Stadsgaard, Danish footballer
- 1985 – Dušan Švento, Slovak footballer
- 1986 – Damien Allen, English footballer
- 1986 – Elijah Kelley, American actor, singer, and dancer
- 1986 – Jonas Plass, German sprinter
- 1986 – Jörn Schlönvoigt, German actor and singer
- 1986 – Lucas Simón, Argentinian footballer
- 1986 – Anton Strålman, Swedish ice hockey player
- 1986 – Andrew Taylor, English footballer
- 1986 – Elena Vesnina, Russian tennis player
- 1986 – Mike Wallace, American football player
- 1987 – Stan, Greek singer-songwriter
- 1987 – Karen Carney, English footballer
- 1987 – Jakov Fak, Croatian-Slovenian biathlete
- 1987 – Rumi Hiiragi, Japanese actress
- 1987 – Sébastien Pocognoli, Belgian footballer
- 1987 – Lee Wallace, Scottish footballer
- 1988 – Mustafa Abdellaoue, Norwegian footballer
- 1988 – Max Carver, American actor
- 1988 – Sasha Jackson, English-American actress
- 1988 – Patryk Małecki, Polish footballer
- 1988 – Bodene Thompson, New Zealand rugby player
- 1988 – Joanna Wang, Taiwanese singer-songwriter

- 1989 – Tiffany, American-South Korean singer, dancer, and actress (Girls' Generation and Girls' Generation-TTS)
- 1989 – Madison Bumgarner, American baseball player
- 1989 – Tomoka Kurokawa, Japanese actress
- 1990 – Aledmys Díaz, Cuban baseball player
- 1990 – Jean Hugues Gregoire, Mauritian swimmer
- 1990 – Elton Jantjies, South African rugby player
- 1990 – Jack O'Connell, English actor
- 1991 – Piotr Malarczyk, Polish footballer
- 1991 – Marco Puntoriere, Italian footballer
- 1992 – Austin Rivers, American basketball player
- 1993 – Álex Abrines, Spanish basketball player
- 1993 – Leon Thomas III, American actor and singer
- 1994 – Sergeal Petersen, South African rugby player
- 1994 – Ayaka Wada, Japanese singer (S/mileage, Hello Pro Kenshūsei, and Shugo Chara Egg!)
- 1995 – Derrick Monasterio, Filipino actor, singer, and dancer
- 1996 – Katie Boulter, English tennis player
- 1996 – Cymphonique Miller, American actress and singer
- 1996 – Ellona Santiago, Filipino-American singer
- 1998 – Khamani Griffin, American actor
- 1999 – Deimantė Kizalaitė, Lithuanian figure skater

Deaths

- 30 BC – Mark Antony, Roman general and politician (b. 83 BC)
- 371 – Eusebius of Vercelli, Italian bishop and saint (b. 283)
- 527 – Justin I, Byzantine emperor (b. 450)
- 946 – Ali ibn Isa al-Jarrah, Abbasid vizier (b. 859)
- 1137 – Louis VI of France (b. 1081)
- 1227 – Shimazu Tadahisa, Japanese warlord (b. 1179)
- 1252 – Giovanni da Pian del Carpine, Italian archbishop and explorer (b. 1180)
- 1402 – Edmund of Langley, 1st Duke of York, English politician, Lord Warden of the Cinque Ports (b. 1341)
- 1457 – Lorenzo Valla, Italian author and educator (b. 1406)
- 1464 – Cosimo de' Medici, Italian ruler (b. 1386)
- 1541 – Simon Grynaeus, German theologian and scholar (b. 1493)
- 1543 – Magnus I, Duke of Saxe-Lauenburg (b. 1488)
- 1557 – Olaus Magnus, Swedish archbishop, historian, and cartographer (b. 1490)
- 1580 – Albrecht Giese, Polish-German politician and diplomat (b. 1524)
- 1589 – Jacques Clément, French assassin of Henry III of France (b. 1567)
- 1714 – Anne, Queen of Great Britain (b. 1665)

- 1787 – Alphonsus Maria de' Liguori, Italian bishop and saint (b. 1696)
- 1795 – Clas Bjerkander, Swedish meteorologist, botanist, and entomologist (b. 1735)
- 1796 – Sir Robert Pigot, 2nd Baronet, English colonel and politician (b. 1720)
- 1798 – François-Paul Brueys d'Aigalliers, French admiral (b. 1753)
- 1807 – John Boorman, English cricketer (b. c. 1754)
- 1807 – John Walker, English actor, philologist, and lexicographer (b. 1732)
- 1812 – Yakov Kulnev, Russian general (b. 1763)
- 1851 – William Joseph Behr, German publicist and academic (b. 1775)
- 1866 – John Ross, American tribal chief (b. 1790)
- 1903 – Calamity Jane, American frontierswoman and scout (b. 1853)
- 1911 – Edwin Austin Abbey, American painter and illustrator (b. 1852)
- 1911 – Samuel Arza Davenport, American lawyer and politician (b. 1843)
- 1918 – John Riley Banister, American cowboy and police officer (b. 1854)
- 1920 – Bal Gangadhar Tilak, Indian lawyer and journalist (b. 1856)
- 1922 – Donát Bánki, Hungarian engineer (b. 1856)
- 1929 – Syd Gregory, Australian cricketer (b. 1870)
- 1938 – John Aasen, American actor (b. 1890)

- 1938 – Edmund C. Tarbell, American painter and academic (b. 1862)
- 1943 – Lydia Litvyak, Russian lieutenant and pilot (b. 1921)
- 1944 – Manuel L. Quezon, Filipino soldier, lawyer, and politician, 2nd President of the Philippines (b. 1878)
- 1945 – Gyula Csortos, Hungarian actor (b. 1883)
- 1959 – Jean Behra, French race car driver (b. 1921)
- 1963 – Theodore Roethke, American poet (b. 1908)
- 1966 – Charles Whitman, American murderer (b. 1941)
- 1967 – Richard Kuhn, Austrian-German biochemist and academic, Nobel Prize Laureate (b. 1900)
- 1970 – Frances Farmer, American actress and singer (b. 1913)
- 1970 – Doris Fleeson, American journalist (b. 1901)
- 1970 – Otto Heinrich Warburg, German physician and physiologist, Nobel Prize laureate (b. 1883)
- 1973 – Gian Francesco Malipiero, Italian composer and educator (b. 1882)
- 1973 – Walter Ulbricht, German soldier and politician (b. 1893)
- 1974 – Ildebrando Antoniutti, Italian cardinal (b. 1898)
- 1977 – Francis Gary Powers, American captain and pilot (b. 1929)
- 1980 – Patrick Depailler, French race car driver (b. 1944)

- 1980 – Strother Martin, American actor (b. 1919)
- 1981 – Paddy Chayefsky, American author, playwright, and screenwriter (b. 1923)
- 1982 – T. Thirunavukarasu, Sri Lankan lawyer and politician (b. 1933)
- 1983 – Lilian Mercedes Letona, Salvadoran activist (b. 1954)
- 1989 – John Ogdon, English pianist and composer (b. 1937)
- 1990 – Norbert Elias, German-Dutch sociologist, author, and academic (b. 1897)
- 1990 – Graham Young, English serial killer (b. 1947)
- 1996 – Mohamed Farrah Aidid, Somalian general and politician, 5th President of Somalia (b. 1934)
- 1996 – Frida Boccara, Moroccan-French singer (b. 1940)
- 1996 – Tadeusz Reichstein, Polish-Swiss chemist and academic, Nobel Prize laureate (b. 1897)
- 1996 – Lucille Teasdale-Corti, Canadian physician and surgeon (b. 1929)
- 1997 – Sviatoslav Richter, Ukrainian pianist (b. 1915)
- 1998 – Eva Bartok, Hungarian-British actress (b. 1927)
- 1999 – Nirad C. Chaudhuri, Bangladeshi–English historian and author (b. 1897)
- 2001 – Korey Stringer, American football player (b. 1974)
- 2003 – Guy Thys, Belgian footballer, coach, and manager (b. 1922)

- 2003 – Marie Trintignant, French actress and screenwriter (b. 1962)
- 2004 – Philip Abelson, American physicist and author (b. 1913)
- 2005 – Al Aronowitz, American journalist (b. 1928)
- 2005 – Wim Boost, Dutch cartoonist and educator (b. 1918)
- 2005 – Constant Nieuwenhuys, Dutch painter and sculptor (b. 1920)
- 2005 – Fahd of Saudi Arabia (b. 1923)
- 2006 – Jason Rhoades, American sculptor (b. 1965)
- 2006 – Ferenc Szusza, Hungarian footballer and manager (b. 1923)
- 2006 – Bob Thaves, American illustrator (b. 1924)
- 2006 – Iris Marion Young, American political scientist and activist (b. 1949)
- 2007 – Tommy Makem, Irish singer-songwriter and banjo player (The Clancy Brothers and Makem and Clancy) (b. 1932)
- 2008 – Gertan Klauber, Czech-English actor (b. 1932)
- 2008 – Harkishan Singh Surjeet, Indian lawyer and politician (b. 1916)
- 2009 – Corazon Aquino, Filipino politician, 11th President of the Philippines (b. 1933)
- 2010 – Lolita Lebrón, Puerto Rican activist (b. 1919)
- 2010 – Eric Tindill, New Zealand rugby player and cricketer (b. 1910)

- 2012 – Aldo Maldera, Italian footballer and agent (b. 1953)
- 2012 – Douglas Townsend, American composer and musicologist (b. 1921)
- 2012 – Barry Trapnell, English cricketer and academic (b. 1924)
- 2013 – John Amis, English journalist and critic (b. 1922)
- 2013 – Chua Boon Huat, Malaysian field hockey player (b. 1980)
- 2013 – Mike Hinton, American guitarist (Rainforest Band) (b. 1956)
- 2013 – Gail Kobe, American actress and producer (b. 1932)
- 2013 – Babe Martin, American baseball player (b. 1920)
- 2013 – Toby Saks, American cellist and educator (b. 1942)
- 2013 – Wilford White, American football player (b. 1928)
- 2014 – Valyantsin Byalkevich, Belarusian footballer and manager (b. 1973)
- 2014 – Rod de'Ath, Welsh drummer and producer (b. 1950)
- 2014 – Michael Johns, Australian-American singer-songwriter (b. 1978)
- 2014 – Jan Roar Leikvoll, Norwegian author (b. 1974)
- 2014 – Charles T. Payne, American soldier (b. 1925)

- 2014 – Mike Smith, English radio and television host (b. 1955)
- 2015 – Stephan Beckenbauer, German footballer and manager (b. 1968)
- 2015 – Cilla Black, English singer and actress (b. 1943)
- 2015 – Bernard d'Espagnat, French physicist, philosopher, and author (b. 1921)
- 2015 – Bob Frankford, English-Canadian physician and politician (b. 1939)
- 2015 – Hong Yuanshuo, Chinese footballer and manager (b. 1948)

Holidays and observances

- Armed Forces Day (Lebanon)
- Armed Forces Day (China) or Anniversary of the Founding of the People's Liberation Army (People's Republic of China)
- Azerbaijani Language and Alphabet Day (Azerbaijan)
- Celebration of the Slavery Abolition Act 1833 which ended the slavery in the British Empire, generally celebrated as a part of Carnival, as the Caribbean Carnival takes place at this time (British West Indies):
  - Earliest day on which Caribana celebration can fall, celebrated on the first Weekend of August. (Toronto)

- Earliest day on which Emancipation Day can fall, celebrated on the first Monday of August. (Anguilla, the Bahamas, British Virgin Islands)
  - Emancipation Day (Barbados, Bermuda, Guyana, Jamaica, Saint Vincent and the Grenadines, Trinidad and Tobago)
- Christian feast day:
  - Abgar V of Edessa (Syrian Church)
  - Alphonsus Maria de' Liguori
  - Æthelwold of Winchester
  - Bernard Võ Văn Duệ (one of Vietnamese Martyrs)
  - Blessed Gerhard Hirschfelder
  - Eusebius of Vercelli
  - Exuperius of Bayeux
  - Felix of Girona
  - Peter Apostle in Chains
  - Procession of the Cross and the beginning of Dormition Fast (Eastern Orthodoxy)
  - The Holy Maccabees
  - August 1 (Eastern Orthodox liturgics)
- Earliest day on which August Bank Holiday (Ireland) can fall, while August 7 is the latest; celebrated on the first Monday of August.
- Earliest day on which Civic Holiday can fall, while August 7 is the latest; celebrated on the first Monday of August. (Canada)

- Earliest day on which Commerce Day, or *Frídagur verslunarmanna*, can fall, while August 7 is the latest; celebrated on the first Monday of August. (Iceland)
- Earliest day on which Farmers' Day can fall, while August 7 is the latest; celebrated on the first Monday of August. (Zambia)
- Earliest day on which International Beer Day can fall, while August 7 is the latest; celebrated on the first Friday of August.
- Earliest day on which International Friendship Day can fall, while August 7 is the latest; celebrated on the first Sunday of August.
- Earliest day on which Kadooment Day can fall, while August 7 is the latest; celebrated on the first Monday of August (Barbados)
- Earliest day on which Labor Day (Samoa) can fall, while August 7 is the latest; celebrated on the first Monday of August (Samoa)
- Feast of Kamál (Perfection); First day of the eighth month of the Bahá'í calendar. (Bahá'í Faith)
- Minden Day (United Kingdom)
- National Day, celebrates the independence of Benin from France in 1960.
- National Day, commemorates Switzerland becoming a single unit in 1291.
- Official Birthday and Coronation Day of the King of Tonga (Tonga)
- Parents' Day (Democratic Republic of the Congo)

- Statehood Day (Colorado)
- The beginning of autumn observances in the Northern hemisphere and spring observances in the Southern hemisphere (Neopagan Wheel of the Year):
  - Lughnasadh in the Northern hemisphere, Imbolc in the Southern hemisphere; traditionally begins on the eve of August 1. (Gaels, Ireland, Scotland, Neopagans)
  - Lammas (England, Scotland, Neopagans)
  - Pachamama Raymi (Quechuan in Ecuador and Peru)
- The first day of Carnaval del Pueblo (Burgess Park, London, England)
- Victory Day (Cambodia, Laos, Vietnam)
- World Scout Scarf Day
- Yorkshire Day (Yorkshire, England)

August fun facts

August is known for many things, including the dog days of summer, National Watermelon Day (Aug. 3) and National Smile Week (Aug. 5-11). But there are many other fun facts associated with summer's last full month.

August is named after Augustus Caesar, founder and the first emperor of the Roman Empire, who was posthumously adopted by his maternal great-uncle Gaius Julius Caesar.

In the early Roman calendar, August was actually the sixth month of the year. It was originally 30 days in length, but an extra day was added so that it would equal the number of days in July, which was named after Julius Caesar.

August has two birthstones: peridot and sardonyx. Peridot is among the oldest known gemstones and is green in color. Sardonyx, which is lesser-known, is a white- and brown-banded gemstone once believed to have mystical powers.

The official flower for August is the gladiolus. These vertical-growing flowers were named from the Latin "gladius," meaning a sword.

Fans of Elvis Presley mourn each Aug. 16th, the day the famed singer died in 1977.

On Aug. 24th in 79 A.D., the volcano Mount Vesuvius erupted, destroying the city of Pompeii and others.

People born in August fall under the sun zodiac signs of Leo and Virgo. Leos are known to be dramatic, creative and outgoing. Virgos have acute attention to detail and are the people most likely to dedicate themselves to serving. They also are loyal, hardworking and analytical.

On Aug. 21, 1911, the Mona Lisa was stolen from the Louvre Gallery and not recovered for two years.

Although civil rights activist Martin Luther King, Jr., is honored in January, when he was born, he is best known for his famed "I have a dream" speech, which was given on Aug. 28, 1963.

The month of August is often referred to as the "dog days of summer" but not because of pet pooches. It has to do with the star Sirius, also known as the dog star, which rose at the same time as sunrise during the month of August in ancient Roman times.

Some famous people born in August include Martha Stewart, Martin Sheen, Jeff Gordon, Deion Sanders and Halle Berry.